I0752584

Contact: leseditions.tossou@gmail.com

1 Photo credit ISTOCK 2220949232

- The Holy Bible, Revised Standard Version, British and Foreign Bible Society, BFBS, 1999.

- The Holy Bible, King James Version, Tenth Printing Hendrickson Publishers Edition, 2019.

French Law No. 49-956 of 16 July 1949 on publications intended for young people

ISBN 978-2-489134-02-5

Legal deposit in France : April 2026

The Great Journey of Froubinou

The path of Joy

VANESSA TOSSOU

Foreword

This book was born out of a simple and profound desire: that every child should be able to know God not only with their head, but above all with their heart.

Through Froubinou's footsteps on the Path of Joy, children are invited to discover that God is present in their daily lives, in their emotions, their questions, their joys and their fears.

Designed for children aged 3 to 10, this book respects their pace, their language and their inner world, using the Bible as a gentle and reliable light to guide them.
It is also intended as a support for parents and church leaders, who are called to accompany the youngest children in their spiritual growth, thanks to clear guidelines and simple tools that can be used in everyday life.
If, through these pages, a child learns to speak to God with confidence, to recognise His peace and to open their Bible with joy, then The Path of Joy will have accomplished its mission. With all my affection.

Vanessa TOSSOU

Contents

The Lane of Feelings

Psalm 139:2 *«Thou knowest when I sit down and when I rise up; thou discernest my thoughts from afar.»*

Froubinou arrives on a little path full of colourful flowers.
He chooses the flower that looks like how he feels inside.
He remembers, «God knows every feeling in my heart.»
His heart grows calm, and the path becomes bright.

Actions

-Say: «Today, I feel...» (name the emotion).
-Make a little face to show an emotion.

Joy

Sadness

Fear

Calm

Anger

The Hideaway of a Peaceful Heart

Joshua 1:9 *«Have I not commanded you? Be strong and of good courage; be not frightened, neither be dismayed; for the Lord your God is with you wherever you go.»*

The wind blows hard, and Froubinou feels worried.

Three little doors open in front of him.

He chooses the one that reminds him that God is always with him.

His heart calms down; he can then continue on his way.

Action

What do you choose to find peace?

The Mountain of Confidence

Psalm 28:7 *«The Lord is my strength and my shield...»*

A steep hill stands before Froubinou.
He thinks he cannot do it.
Each step has words written on it:
«God gives me strength.»
«I keep believing.»
In his head, he says:
«Jesus gives me strength to keep going.»
His heart becomes courageous.
Froubinou reaches the summit.
He thanks God for helping him.

Action

- Say: «I try again.»

Remember that Jesus is with you and will help you.

God
gives me
strength.
I keep
believing

The Garden of Patience

Psalm 40:1 *«I waited patiently for the Lord; he inclined to me and heard my cry.»*

Froubinou has planted a tiny seed.
He looks at the soil... nothing moves.
He wishes the flower would grow straight away.
To help the seed, Froubinou waters it gently.
Then he whispers: «I can wait.»

When he stays calm, a very small bud appears.
Then he says, «God makes things grow at the right time.»

Action

Plant a seed and water it gently each day.

The forest of sharing

Acts 20:35 *«... It is more blessed to give than to receive.»*

Froubinou finds lots of red apples.
Some escape from his paws.
He remembers: «There is more joy in giving than in receiving.»
He gives one to the squirrels.
His heart shines.The path becomes more and more beautiful. Sharing makes the heart happy.

Actions

-Give a gift to someone.
-Share your toys with friends, your brother, or your sister.

The Path of Gentleness

Proverbs 15:1 *«A soft answer turns away wrath...»*

A little grey cloud follows **Froubinou**.

He frowns, and his heart feels tight.

A Bible verse comes back to his heart:

«Gentleness calms anger.»

He breathes slowly, shakes his ears, and whispers:

«I choose peace.»

The cloud fades, and light returns to the path.

Actions

-Breathe slowly when anger rises.
-Say softly: «I choose peace, because Jesus gives me his peace.»

The Hill of Joy

Nehemiah 8:10 *«... for the joy of the Lord is your strength.»*
Froubinou feels tired and floppy.
He does not know why.
He remembers,
«The joy of the Lord fills my heart.»
Colourful bubbles float into the air.
He touches the brightest ones.
They burst into light.
He laughs. He jumps.
His heart feels light again.
He walks on happily.
A golden path appears.

Actions

-Jump three times saying : «Yippee!» while thinking of something you love.
-Look at God's creation: the sky, the birds, the clouds...

The Trail of Truth

Psalm 119:105 *«Thy word is a lamp to my feet and a light to my path.»*

Froubinou accidentally knocks over a pot of seeds.
He does not want to be told off.
He does not know what to do.
Three doors stand before him:
The truth... Hiding... Changing the subject.
Froubinou chooses to tell the truth
and opens the right door.
The others stay closed.
Light comes back when he tells the truth.
Behind the door, a village appears.

Action

Tell the truth each day, even when it is difficult.

The truth
Hiding
Changing the subject

The Village of Kindness

1 John 3:18 *«Little children, let us not love in word or speech bet in deed and in truth.»*

A little bird lies on the ground, very tired.
Froubinou comes closer, gently helping.
He shares some bread and brings fresh water.
Froubinou remembers: «To love is to help.»
The bird flies away again.
Froubinou walks on, happy.

Actions

- Help Mum or Dad tidy up at home.
- Say a kind word to your brother or sister.

The Door of Listening

Proverbs 4:20 *«My son, be attentive to my words; incline your ear to my sayings.»*

There is a lot of noise around Froubinou, and he feels disturbed. He closes his eyes, listens to a sound, then a melody.

In his heart, Froubinou understands that God speaks constantly. And that, when you become calm inside, it is easier to hear His voice even in the midst of noise.

In the calm, Froubinou's heart opens to God and the door lights up.

Actions

-Take a moment of silence.
-Close your eyes for a few seconds.
-Say softly: «Lord, i am listening.»

The Victory

Froubinou comes out of the maze and jumps with joy: he has won!

A great heart-shaped light surrounds Froubinou.

Message for the Child

You have won too!

Read your Bible often - it will help you each day to make good choices.

"God promises joy, peace, and protection to those who follow His ways."

Appendix 1 — Guide for Parents & Church Leaders

Guide your child (aged three to ten) on the Path of Joy.

This guide helps adults connect each step of Froubinou's journey with an important spiritual need of the child. The chapters are not just stories - they become simple tools to help a child's heart grow each day.

1.Feeling Known and Loved by God

Key need: Discovering that God knows and loves the child personally.

Chapter: The Lane of Feelings

The child learns that all their feelings are known by God. Saying how they feel, making a face, choosing a flower — all of this helps them understand they can be honest with God without fear.

Adult's role: Welcome the emotion without correcting it. Simply say, "God knows how you feel, and He loves you."

2. Finding Peace and Safety in God

Key need: Feeling reassured and protected.

Chapter: The Hideaway of a Peaceful Heart

When worried, Froubinou chooses God's presence. The child learns that peace can come through a simple choice.

Adult's role: Name the fear, then gently remind them, "God is with you."

3. Receiving Strength and Trust to Keep Going

Key need: Learning that God helps when things are hard.

Chapter: The Mountain of Confidence

Each step shares a simple truth: God gives strength. The child learns they can try again.
Adult's role: Encourage effort rather than results. Praise perseverance.

4. Learning Patience and God's Timing
Key need: Understanding that not everything comes straight away.
Chapter: The Garden of patience
The slowly growing seed shows God's timing in a way children can see.
Adult's role: Show that waiting can be calm and trusting.

5. Discovering the Joy of Giving and Sharing
Key need: Growing in generosity.
Chapter: The Forest of sharing
Sharing brings joy and makes the path more beautiful.
Adult's role: Value every act of sharing, even small ones.

6. Choosing Gentleness and Peace
Key need: Learning how to handle anger.
Chapter: The Path of gentleness
Breathing, speaking softly, choosing peace – the child discovers another way to respond.
Adult's role: Lead by example, with a calm voice and gentle actions.

7. Living Joy as a Strength
Key need: The joy of the Lord gives strength.
Chapter: The Hill of Joy

Joy is lived through the body: jumping, laughing, smiling.
Adult's role: Encourage joyful expression and daily gratitude.

8. Understanding the Importance of Truth

Key need: Truth lights the path and opens the right door.
Chapter: The Trail of Truth
Adult's role: Reassure the child that truth brings light, not rejection.

9. Learning to Love Through Actions

Key need: Understanding kindness in real ways.
Chapter: The Village of Kindness
Helping, sharing, caring — love is shown through simple actions.
Adult's role: Highlight loving actions in everyday life.

10. Learning to Listen to God

Key need: Discovering inner calm and listening.
Chapter: The Door of Listening
Inner quiet opens the heart. The child learns that God speaks all the time.
Adult's role: Create short moments of peaceful silence.

Final Message — Victory

The child understands they are never alone: God's Word guides their path.
Adult's role: Often remind them that walking with God brings joy, peace, and protection.

Appendix 2 — 10 Christian Family Activities

1. Have an evening prayer time with a simple sentence to repeat together.

2. Read an illustrated Bible story once a week.

3. Make a family gratitude notebook.

4. Draw a picture of "God protects me" to display in the bedroom.

5.Sing a Christian song or hymn in the morning.

6.Act out positive Bible scenes together.

7. Create a "kindness jar" for little notes of love.

8 Go for a nature walk and talk about God's creation.

9. Hold a short family worship time on Sunday morning.

10. Build a Bible puzzle or do a craft inspired by a Bible verse.

We are committed to protecting the environment.
This book has been printed in accordance with biodiversity regulations.

www.ingramcontent.com/pod-product-compliance
Lightning Source LLC
LaVergne TN
LVHW070203110826
845147LV00002B/491

* 9 7 8 2 4 8 9 1 3 4 0 2 5 *